FATHER'S DAY

BY ANN HEINRICHS · ILLUSTRATED BY R. W. ALLEY

Published in the United States of America by The Child's World®
PO Box 326 • Chanhassen, MN 55317-0326
800-599-READ • www.childsworld.com

ACKNOWLEDGMENTS
The Child's World®: Mary Berendes, Publishing Director

Editorial Directions, Inc.: E. Russell Primm, Editorial Director; Katie Marsico, Managing Editor; Judith Shiffer, Assistant Editor; Caroline Wood and Rory Mabin, Editorial Assistants; Susan Hindman, Copy Editor and Proofreader; Elizabeth Nellums, Rory Mabin, Ruth Martin, and Caroline Wood, Fact Checkers; Tim Griffin/IndexServ, Indexer

The Design Lab: Kathleen Petelinsek, Design and Page Production

LIBRARY OF CONGRESS CATALOGING-IN-PUBLICATION DATA
Heinrichs, Ann.
 Father's Day / by Ann Heinrichs ; illustrated by R. W. Alley.
  p. cm. — (Holidays, festivals, & celebrations)
 Includes index.
 ISBN 1-59296-575-X (lib. bdg. : alk. paper)
 1. Father's Day—Juvenile literature. I. Alley, R. W. (Robert W.), ill. II. Title. III. Series.
 HQ756.5.H45 2006
 394.263—dc22   2005025682

TABLE OF CONTENTS

CHAPTER ONE

HAPPY FATHER'S DAY!

I'm just as lucky as I can be
For the world's best Dad belongs to me!
—Author unknown

You may call him Daddy, Papa, Father, or Dad. He is strong, wise, and fun. Best of all, he loves you. We have a special holiday just for him. It's Father's Day!

That day, we thank fathers for all they do. We also honor those who are like fathers to us. They may be grandfathers, stepfathers, uncles, or big brothers. They might even be neighbors or family friends.

What's the best way to say "Happy Father's Day"? Just say, "I love you!"

Father's Day is a time to say thank you to dads and to all those in our lives who are like dads to us.

CHAPTER TWO

THE FIRST FATHER'S DAY CARD

A story is told about a boy named Elmesu. He lived almost four thousand years ago. His home was in Mesopotamia (mess-oh-poh-TAY-mee-uh). Part of this **ancient** region is in modern Iraq.

Elmesu made a tablet of wet clay. Using a **reed**, he carefully carved a message on it. He wished his father health. And he wished him a long life.

Elmesu didn't know what he had done. He had made the first Father's Day card!

A wise son makes a glad father.
—The Bible, Proverbs 10:1

Elmesu wrote the first Father's Day card thousands of years ago.

Blessed indeed is the man
who hears many gentle
voices call him father!
—Lydia M. Child
(1802–1880)

CHAPTER THREE

HOW DID FATHER'S DAY BEGIN?

Who started Father's Day? A loving daughter! Her name was Sonora Smart Dodd. Sonora grew up on a farm in Washington State in the early 1900s. Her mother died when she was little. Sonora's father, William Smart, was left with six children. He raised them all by himself.

One Mother's Day, Sonora was in church. The **sermon** was about mothers. But Sonora couldn't help thinking about her father. He had been so strong and loving. Suddenly, she had an idea. Why not have a Father's Day?

William Smart raised six children on his own.

In the United States,
Father's Day is celebrated on
the third Sunday in June.

William Smart's birthday was in June. So Sonora suggested a Sunday in June. Her church agreed to hold a service for fathers that day. It was held on June 19, 1910. That was the first Father's Day celebration.

The idea spread quickly. Soon people around the country were celebrating Father's Day. At last, it was made a permanent **national** holiday in 1972.

Father's Day became an official holiday in 1972.

BE KIND

Be kind to thy father, for
when thou wert young,
Who loved thee so
fondly as he?
He caught the first accents
that fell from thy
tongue,
And joined in thy
innocent glee.
—Margaret Courtney

CHAPTER FOUR

HOW DO WE CELEBRATE?

We celebrate Father's Day by showing dads how much we love them!

There are many Father's Day **traditions.** One is giving Father's Day cards. Inside the cards are warm and loving messages.

We might have a special dinner just for Dad. Or treat him to his favorite activity. Or give him a gift that has something to do with his hobby. There's one gift he's sure to love. It's a great big hug!

Many people wear a rose on Father's Day. A red rose means the father is living. A white rose means he has died. But a child's love lives forever.

Does your dad like fishing? A Father's Day fishing trip might be a good way to celebrate his special day!

DADDY, I LOVE YOU

Daddy, I love you
For all that you do.
I'll kiss you and hug you
'Cause you love me, too.

You feed me and need me
To teach you to play,
So smile 'cause I love you
On this Father's Day.
—Author unknown

CHAPTER FIVE

FATHERS OF ALL KINDS

W hat kinds of fathers are there? All kinds! Just look at George Washington. He's called the Father of Our Country. Other great men helped form the United States. We call them the Founding Fathers. Albert Einstein was a famous scientist. He helped us understand space and time. We have a name for him, too.

George Washington was a father to the new United States.

He's often called the Father of Modern Science.

Some of these men had no children. Yet we look up to them as fathers. They helped us by leading, guiding, and teaching. They were all great fathers to us!

Albert Einstein fathered many of the important ideas in modern science.

CHAPTER SIX

FATHER'S DAY AROUND THE WORLD

People around the world have a special day for fathers. In many Christian countries, it's March 19. That's Saint Joseph's Day. Joseph was the husband of Mary, Jesus's mother. Joseph lovingly raised Jesus. He became a model for caring fathers.

In Taiwan, Father's Day is August 8. That date—8/8—is pronounced BA BA in Chinese. And *baba* is Chinese for "father!"

Father's Day is a winter holiday in Sweden. It's the second Sunday in November. Fathers get

My heart is happy,
my mind is free.
I had a father who
talked with me.
—Hilda Bigelow

Father's Day is celebrated on August 8 in Taiwan.

Safe, for a child, is his
father's hand, holding
him tight.
—Marion C. Garretty
(1917–)

a special cake that day. Children make drawings for their fathers. Some even serve their father breakfast in bed!

Swedish fathers sometimes get breakfast in bed on Father's Day.

CHAPTER SEVEN

THE POETS' CORNER

Daddy's Footsteps

"Walk a little slower, Daddy,"
Said a little child so small.
"I'm following in your footsteps,
And I don't want to fall.

"Sometimes your steps are very fast,
Sometimes they're hard to see;
So walk a little slower, Daddy,
For you are leading me.

"Someday when I'm all grown up,
You're what I want to be;
Then I will have a little child
Who'll want to follow me.

"And I would want to lead just right,
And know that I was true;
So walk a little slower, Daddy,
For I must follow you!"

—Author unknown

What Is a Dad?

A dad is a person who's loving and kind,
And often he knows what you have on your mind.

He's someone who listens, suggests, and defends—
A dad can be one of your very best friends!

He's proud of your triumphs, but when things go wrong,
A dad can be patient and helpful and strong.

In all that you do, a dad's love plays a part—
There's always a place for him deep in your heart.

And each year that passes, you're even more glad,
More grateful and proud just to call him your dad!

—Author unknown

Our Fathers

Our fathers toil with hands and heart
To make our lives complete.
They quietly brave the winter cold,
Endure the summer heat.

Our fathers' lives are busy, but
There's always time for us.
They boldly face the ups and downs
And seldom ever fuss.

Our fathers are the greatest dads.
We know you know this, too.
But thank you for the chance to share
Our love for them with you.

—Author unknown

CHAPTER EIGHT

OUR GRANDFATHERS AND UNCLES

Walking with Grandpa

I like to walk with Grandpa,
His steps are short like mine.
He doesn't say, "Now hurry up!"
He always takes his time.

I like to walk with Grandpa,
His eyes see things like mine do—
Wee pebbles bright, a funny cloud,
Half hidden drops of dew.

Children's children are the crown of old men.
—The Bible, Proverbs 17:6

Most people have to hurry,
They do not stop and see.
I'm glad that God made Grandpa
Unrushed and young like me.

—*Author unknown*

Grown men can learn from very little children, for the hearts of little children are pure.
—*Nicholas Black Elk (1863–1950)*

My Uncle

My uncle's very special—
He's warm and kind, you see.
No matter when I need to talk,
He has time for me.

He teaches me what's right and wrong
And shows me how to be.
He treasures having me around
Just because I'm me.

Thank you, Uncle _____,
For the loving things you do.
I hope that I'll grow up to be
As wonderful as you!

—Author unknown

You can tell your uncle stuff that you could not tell your dad.
—Dusty Baker
(1949–)

Showing Our Love on *Father's Day*

- What's your father's favorite meal? Burgers or a steak? Why not have another adult help you cook it for him?

- Do you have a special grandfather, stepfather, or uncle? Show your love by giving him a nice card.

- Do you know someone from another country? Ask if he or she celebrates a special holiday for fathers. Ask what the holiday customs are.

- Is there a home for older people in your community? See if you can visit on Father's Day. Bring cards or flowers for the men. Ask them to tell you about their lives.

Making a Portrait from Vegetables, Cheese, and Crackers

Ingredients:
2 cherry tomatoes
1 orange
1 ounce cheddar cheese
8 thin wheat crackers (square or rectangular crackers work best)
¼ cup shredded carrot

Directions:
Slice the cherry tomatoes in half, and peel and divide the orange. Cut the cheese into a variety of shapes, including squares, triangles, and circles.* Arrange the crackers on a plate so they form a rectangle or square. Use the cheese, tomatoes, orange, and carrots to design your dad's face on the crackers. Two tomato halves can be his eyes, and the shredded carrot is good for hair. Turn an orange slice right side up or upside down to make a smile or frown. Pick a cheese shape that looks most like your dad's nose. Mix and match the ingredients to form different features. Get creative—you could make a face for every member of your family!

Have an adult (especially a dad) help you with the cutting.

Making a Photo House

*This project is sure to bring a smile to Dad's face when
he sees a house filled with all his favorite people!*

What you need:

1 sheet of white construction
    paper or other heavyweight
    paper

Crayons or markers

1 photo of each member of your
    family

1 piece of cardboard about the
    same size as your sheet of paper

Scissors

Tape

Glue

Instructions:

1. Use crayons or markers to draw your house on the sheet of white paper. Draw a window for each member of your family.
2. Cut out the window openings with the scissors. Ask an adult to help with this step.
3. Place a photo behind each window and tape it in place along the edges.
4. Use the scissors to cut out the outline of the house.
5. Place the cutout house face down on the table.
6. Spread glue along the outside edges of the house and place the cardboard on top of the house.
7. Let the glue dry.
8. Ask an adult to help you trim the cardboard so it is the same size as the house.

Now you're ready to present your dad with a special gift. Happy Father's Day!

Words to Know

ancient (*AYN-shunt*) very old; often meaning thousands of years old

national (*NASH-uh-nuhl*) relating to a country

reed (*REED*) the stiff stem of a tall grass that grows along the edge of lakes

sermon (*SIR-muhn*) a speech given in church that teaches a lesson

stepfathers (*STEP-fah-thurz*) men who become fathers after marrying women who already have children

traditions (*truh-DISH-unz*) long-held customs

How to Learn More about Father's Day

At the Library

Berenstain, Stan, and Jan Berenstain. *The Berenstain Bears and the Papa's Day Surprise.* New York: Random House, 2003.

London, Jonathan, and Frank Remkiewicz (illustrator). *Froggy's Day with Dad.* New York: Viking, 2004.

Plourde, Lynne, and Amy Wummer. *Dad, Aren't You Glad?* New York: Dutton Children's Books, 2005.

Robinson, Fay. *Father's Day Crafts.* Berkeley Heights, N.J.: Enslow Elementary, 2005.

On the Web

Visit our home page for lots of links about Father's Day:
http://www.childsworld.com/links
NOTE TO PARENTS, TEACHERS, AND LIBRARIANS:
We routinely verify our Web links to make sure they're safe,
active sites—so encourage your readers to check them out!

ABOUT THE AUTHOR

Ann Heinrichs lives in Chicago, Illinois. She has written more than two hundred books for children. She loves traveling to faraway places.

ABOUT THE ILLUSTRATOR

R. W. Alley enjoys drawing pictures of happy families from his home in Rhode Island. He's guided in this effort by his winsome wife and two cheery children.

Index